THE WORLD OF SILENCE

SO-AIM-279

CONTENTS

Introduction 2

How Sounds Travel to the Brain 3

Types of Hearing Loss 5

Hearing Aids 10

Forms of Communication 14

Education for Hearing-Impaired Children 20

Everyday Life for the Hearing Impaired 22

Other Ways of Hearing 28

The Deaf Community 30

Written by Catherine Harold

INTRODUCTION

Hearing is one of the five senses. The other senses are sight, smell, taste, and touch. When people suffer from hearing loss they lose the ability to hear sound. People can range from being profoundly deaf, which means they cannot hear any sound at all, to losing the ability to hear even quiet noises. People can be born deaf or they can become deaf at some stage in their life.

Hearing is a complex process. All moving things make sounds. Sounds are made by vibrations that move in waves, called sound waves. For people to hear, sound waves must enter the outer ear and move through the middle and inner ear. They are then sent to the brain so that they can be turned into sounds. Any kind of blockage or damage along this passage from the outer ear to the brain may cause some degree of hearing loss.

Deafness or partial deafness has a huge impact on a person's life. It can affect language development, education, and many aspects of everyday living. Fortunately, there are many ways that deaf and hearing people can address these problems. These will be explored later in this book.

HOW SOUNDS TRAVEL TO THE BRAIN

For people to hear sounds, sound waves have first to enter the outer ear. These waves hit the eardrum, causing it to vibrate. The vibrations then travel through three small bones in the middle ear called auditory ossicles.

The auditory ossicles have Latin names, *malleus*, which means *hammer*, *incus*, which means *anvil*, and *stapes*, which means *stirrup*. The bones were given these names because they look like a hammer, an anvil, and a stirrup.

The malleus is the biggest bone in the middle ear. It is connected to the eardrum at one end and onto the incus at the other. The stapes is the smallest bone in the body, smaller even than a grain of rice. The stapes is joined to a membrane called the oval window. The oval window leads to the inner ear. When the footplate of the stapes vibrates, it creates waves in the fluid that fills a part of the inner ear called the cochlea. Inside the cochlea is a membrane that is covered with thousands of tiny hairs. As the fluid touches these hairs, they bend. As they bend, they create impulses in nerve cells that are attached to the base of the hairs. The cochlear nerve transmits these impulses to the temporal lobe, the hearing center of the brain. The brain interprets these impulses as sound.

The intensity of the sound depends on how many impulses are sent to the brain. Large sounds move large numbers of hairs, so the cochlear nerve sends many impulses to the brain. Soft sounds move fewer hairs so fewer impulses are sent to the brain.

Outer and Inner Ear

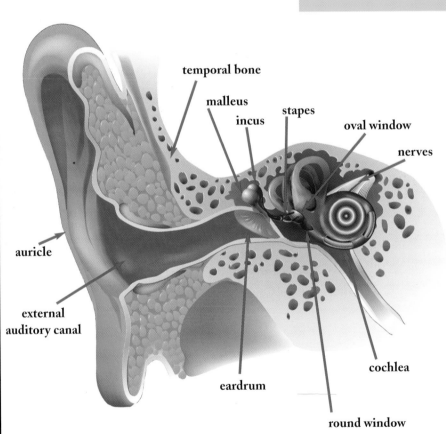

temporal bone

malleus

incus

stapes

oval window

nerves

auricle

external auditory canal

eardrum

cochlea

round window

TYPES OF HEARING LOSS

There are two main types of hearing loss. These are conductive hearing loss and sensorineural hearing loss. Conductive hearing loss occurs when there is damage or a blockage to the outer or middle ear. This means that sound cannot be conducted to the inner ear. Sensorineural hearing loss occurs when there is damage in the inner ear, or damage to the auditory nerve, which is the nerve that leads from the inner ear to the brain. This means that sound cannot be interpreted. Sensorineural hearing loss is more common than conductive hearing loss and usually irreversible.

People can also suffer from mixed hearing loss. In cases of mixed hearing loss, there are problems in both the conduction and interpretation of sound.

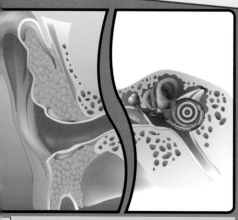

Where conductive hearing loss occurs

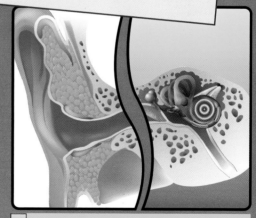

Where sensorineural hearing loss occurs

There are many causes of hearing loss. Aging is the most common cause of hearing loss. Some birth defects and diseases may cause deafness. People can also lose their hearing due to factors in the environment.

AGING

As people get older, their hearing can become damaged. Age-related hearing loss comes on slowly and gets worse. There is no cure for this type of hearing loss.

BIRTH DEFECTS

Birth defects are a well-known cause of many cases of sensorineural deafness.

People who are born deaf, or go deaf later in life for no apparent reason, have most likely inherited a gene that causes deafness. This type of deafness is called genetic deafness.

Another reason why people are born deaf or go deaf later in life is that something has gone wrong before, or soon after, they were born. For example, a mother who has had a disease called rubella when she was first pregnant may give birth to a deaf baby. This type of deafness is called congenital deafness. Another example of congenital deafness would be where an unborn baby had a substance in its blood called the Rh factor.

If the Rh factor is not in the mother's blood, the mother's body reacts. This may lead the baby to be born deaf.

DISEASES

Diseases can cause both conductive and sensorineural hearing loss. The main cause of conductive hearing loss is a disease called otitis media. Otitis media is a disease in the middle ear. Children often get this disease. If it is not treated promptly, it can lead to deafness. Children also get diseases that cause a high fever. High fevers can damage the inner ear and the auditory nerve.

Another disease that can cause deafness is one that causes a growth around the stapes. This stops the vibrations getting to the inner ear.

A disease that affects millions of older people is called Meniers disease. This disorder upsets a person's balance and can also lead to deafness.

ENVIRONMENTAL FACTORS

Many factors in the environment can cause hearing loss. These include a blow to the head or ear, loud noises, and objects stuck in the ear. Even something as simple as a build-up in earwax can cause hearing loss.

Some loud noises like explosions can cause people to become deaf. Sometimes their hearing comes back later on. Other noises, like listening to very loud music for years, can also damage hearing. There is no cure for this type of hearing loss. But it can be avoided.

Some Causes of Deafness

Cause of Deafness	Prevention	Treatment
Foreign object in ear	Keep small objects away from ears	Remove
Excessive wax	Clean ears regularly	Soften wax with oil. Flush out with warm water.
Loud music over time	Turn down the volume	No known cure. Wear a hearing aid. Learn to sign and lip read.
Working with noisy tools and equipment	Wear earmuffs	No known cure. Wear a hearing aid. Learn to sign and lip read.
Explosions	Wear earmuffs if explosion is predictable	No known cure. Time may reverse deafness. Wear a hearing aid. Learn to sign and lip read.
Blows to the head or ear	Wear hard hats in situations that could result in blows to the head	No known cure. Time may reverse deafness. Wear a hearing aid. Learn to sign and lip read.

Some Causes of Deafness

Cause of Deafness	Prevention	Treatment
Diseases with high fever	Keep fever down by keeping body cool. Seek medical advice as soon as possible, especially if fever is caused by a complication of a common disease like measles.	No known cure. Wear a hearing aid. Learn to sign and lip read.
Meniers disease		No known cure. Wear a hearing aid. Learn to sign and lip read.
Genetic factors		No known cure, but cochlea implants may help. Wear a hearing aid where possible. Learn to sign and lip read.
Congenital factors	Avoid risk situations where possible. See a doctor promptly if exposed to risks, for example, rubella in the first three months of pregnancy.	No known cure, but cochlea implants may help. Wear a hearing aid where possible. Learn to sign and lip read.
Aging	Avoid risk situations throughout life	No known cure. Wear a hearing aid where possible. Learn to sign and lip read.

HEARING AIDS

There are many things people can use to help them hear. Hearing aids are the most common. Hearing aids do not restore a person's hearing. But a hearing aid can improve hearing and help with day-to-day living.

These tiny aids amplify sounds. Hearing aids can be tuned to different frequencies. For example, if a person has trouble hearing low sounds, their hearing aid can be tuned to amplify low sounds. But hearing aids amplify all sounds on a frequency – and not just the one the person needs to hear. So if a person cannot hear people talking, the aid will amplify background voices as well as the voice of the person speaking. This can be very distracting.

Hearing aids cannot be tuned to amplify all frequencies at once. So there are often gaps in what a person hears. The sound can also be distorted. But hearing aids can enable hearing-impaired people to do many things that they could not do without them, such as listen to music and talk on the telephone.

DIFFERENT TYPES OF HEARING AIDS

There are many different types of hearing aids. A person will choose a hearing aid based on the kind of help needed, what it looks like, and the price.

In days gone by, hearing aids were bulky objects. Eyeglass hearing aids and body hearing aids were two of the first hearing aids. Eyeglass hearing aids were fixed to the side of a person's eyeglasses. Wires ran from the eyeglasses to the person's ear. This kind of hearing aid was useful only to people who wore glasses. The hearing aids were useless as soon as the person took the glasses off.

Body aids were worn somewhere on the body. They were also connected to the ears with wires. Some people, particularly children with severe hearing loss, still wear body hearing aids today.

Modern hearing aids have five main parts. Three parts are to do with receiving the sound. These parts are a microphone, an amplifier, and a receiver. The other two parts are a battery and an earmold. The microphone picks up the sound and changes it into impulses. The amplifier amplifies the strength of the impulses. The receiver then changes the amplified impulses back into sound. The battery powers the aid and the earmold holds the aid in place.

Modern hearing aids fit behind or in the ear. Behind-the-ear aids have earmolds that fit behind a person's ears. Earmolds are connected to the hearing aid with wires. Behind-the-ear aids provide more amplification than other styles. This is because they have large batteries and strong amplifiers.

In-the-ear hearing aids are smaller than behind-the-ear aids. They fit into the opening of the ear so they are harder to see.

In-the-canal hearing aids are almost invisible. They fit into the space at the beginning of the ear canal or right into the ear canal. Because they are so small, the amplifier and battery are also small. People with mild hearing loss wear these aids. They do not amplify sound enough for people very hard of hearing.

Some hearing aids have a computer chip inside. This makes it easier to tune the aid to a user's needs. Some of these aids have different settings. The user is able to adjust the settings. For example, a child using an aid with a computer chip can change the settings from "in the car" to "in the classroom."

Some people are so deaf that hearing aids do not help them. Cochlear implants can help these people to hear certain sounds. A cochlear implant is an electrode that is put into, or next to, the cochlea. The cochlear implant does not amplify sounds like a hearing aid. It takes over some of the functions of the damaged cochlea. It translates sounds into impulses and delivers them to the auditory nerve.

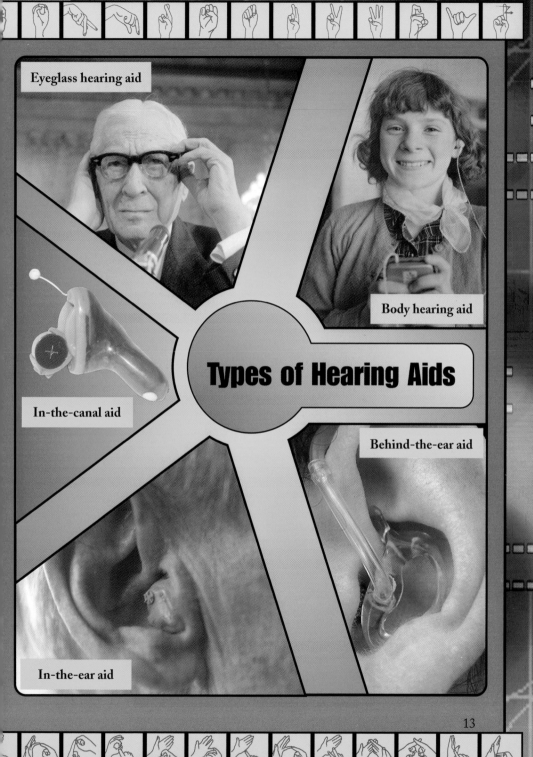

Eyeglass hearing aid

Body hearing aid

In-the-canal aid

Types of Hearing Aids

Behind-the-ear aid

In-the-ear aid

FORMS OF COMMUNICATION

When people suffer from hearing loss it can affect their language development. If people are born profoundly deaf, they will never hear anyone speak. This makes it hard for them to copy the speech of others. Profoundly deaf people may find it so hard to talk with other people that they do not try to talk at all. It is easy for these people to feel lonely or left out.

However, there are many ways for profoundly deaf people to communicate. Some people lip read or use sign language. Others use an interpreter. Many use a combination of these.

Sign language is a common form of communication used by deaf people.

LIP READING

Lip reading is much more than just reading someone's lips. People also need to read facial expressions and gestures. Lip reading is about 70 percent guesswork for deaf people. Even if someone speaks clearly, a lot of the lip patterns for different letters are the same. If people have been profoundly deaf from birth, or from a very young age, lip reading is even harder. They have to lip read a language that they have never heard before. It is like trying to understand a foreign language the first time you hear it.

Making Lip Reading Easier

- Face the deaf person.

- Make sure you have their attention.

- Ensure that they can see your face.

- Make sure there is no background noise if the person is wearing a hearing aid.

- Tell the person what you are talking about. This will make it easier to understand from the start what you are saying.

- Speak clearly and slowly.

- Make sure the person understands what you said before you move on.

- Use different words to say it again if you are not being understood.

- Keep your voice down. Do not shout. It does not help. In fact it makes it worse. Shouting distorts your lip patterns.

- Point to things when you talk about them whenever you can.

- Use gestures such as nodding, when the other person speaks.

- Write down what you are saying if you are stuck.

SIGN LANGUAGES

Sign languages are languages without spoken words. Sign languages combine hand and arm signs with facial expressions and body movements. Sign languages have rules just like spoken and written languages.

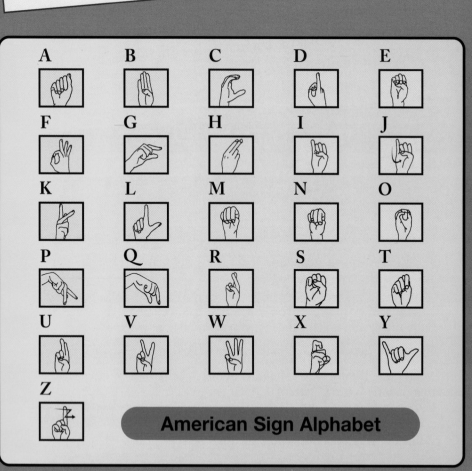

American Sign Alphabet

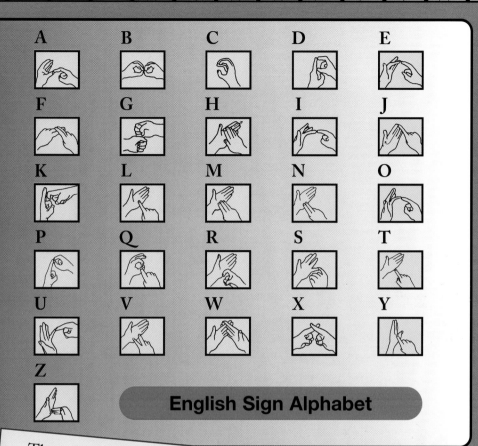

English Sign Alphabet

There are many sign languages used around the world. In the English language there is a British Sign Language (BSL) and an American Sign Language (ASL). People using the same sign language may sign things differently depending on where they live. This is just the same as people who all speak one language, but say things in a different way depending on where they live.

Learning sign language is like learning to talk for children born deaf. Deaf children born to deaf parents learn sign language from their parents. They learn language at the same rate as hearing children born to hearing parents. Deaf children born to hearing parents may acquire language more slowly because the parents have to learn sign language, too. Most hearing people do not know how to use sign language.

Learning sign language is like learning a foreign language for people who develop deafness later in life. These people are less likely to sign because they think it is too difficult to learn a new language.

Group of deaf friends holding a conversation in sign language

Some people in the deaf community believe that deaf people should learn to use a spoken language. They say that using only sign language keeps them from communicating with hearing people. Other people in the deaf community believe that sign language provides deaf people with a way to communicate, and that they should not be forced to adapt to the hearing world.

INTERPRETERS

Interpreters provide a crucial link between hearing people and deaf people.

Sign-language interpreters can quickly translate spoken words into sign language. They interpret the deaf person's signs and then speak them aloud to the hearing person. They also interpret plays, songs, and other public performances.

EDUCATION FOR HEARING-IMPAIRED CHILDREN

Children learn to speak from what they hear. They learn the meanings of words through experience. If children cannot hear, it affects their development. So it is important to test a baby's hearing. That way any possible hearing loss can be detected early.

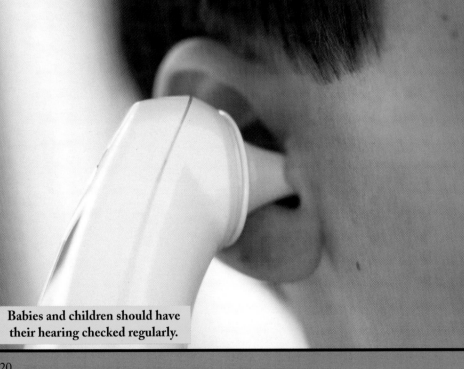

Babies and children should have their hearing checked regularly.

Children with an unidentified hearing problem may fall behind in school. These children may miss information. They may not hear all of a teacher's directions or questions. However, if the hearing loss is identified, a hearing-impaired or profoundly deaf child will do fine in school.

There are many things that can be done to assist hearing-impaired children in the classroom. Most of these are very simple. The teacher can write instructions on the board as well as telling children what to do. Having a hearing-impaired child sit in the front row can help cut out background noise. Making sure that people look at the child as they speak can help them lip read. Teachers and other classmates can learn sign language. Sometimes tutors or interpreters can help.

Hearing-impaired and profoundly deaf children can also be taught at special schools for the deaf.

Deaf children learning in sign language

EVERYDAY LIFE FOR THE HEARING IMPAIRED

Many deaf people have found ways that make it easier for them to live alone. They can live independently because they can now hear by seeing things. Some people turn up the volume on devices such as telephones, smoke alarms, and doorbells. Others fit lights to these devices so they flash when in use.

USING THE TELEPHONE

Many deaf people turn up the volume control on their telephones. This helps them hear it ring and hear the person who is talking. Sometimes people also fit a light to their telephones. When the phone rings, the light flashes. This tells the person that someone is calling them. Some cell phones can be set to vibrate rather than ring. When someone calls, the phone vibrates letting the owner know that there is a call to answer.

When telephone numbers are listed for businesses, sometimes there is a separate phone number with the initials TTY or TTD listed next to it. Both TTY and TTD enable deaf people to use the telephone. Many people call this a text telephone.

Text telephone services help link hearing-impaired people with the world. A special relay service provides the link. If a hearing person calls through a TTD or TTY number, an operator will come on the line. The operator will type everything the person says. This could be the person's name and why they are calling. The person on the other end will see a written display of the words. That person can then type back a reply. The operator will read the reply back.

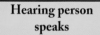
Hearing person speaks

Operator types hearing persons's words

Deaf person reads what operator has typed

Hearing person listens to operator

Operator reads deaf person's response to hearing person

Deaf person types a response

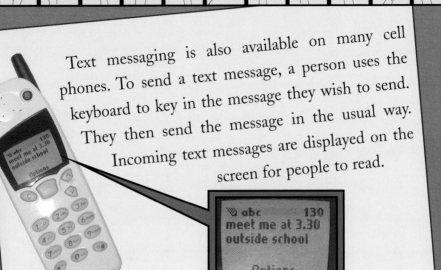

Text messaging is also available on many cell phones. To send a text message, a person uses the keyboard to key in the message they wish to send. They then send the message in the usual way. Incoming text messages are displayed on the screen for people to read.

E-MAIL

The advent of the Internet and e-mail has made it easy for people to communicate with others all over the world. This is especially true for deaf people. The Internet and e-mail provide an alternative to the telephone.

The Internet and e-mail make communication easy for deaf people.

CLOSED CAPTION TV

A significant number of people in every country are hard of hearing. In the United States of America alone there are an estimated 20 million people who cannot understand everything they see on television because they cannot hear. Closed captioning makes it possible for those people to more fully enjoy TV shows.

A caption is a text under a picture. Books often have captions under photographs and illustrations. The captions describe what is happening. On television programs, captions are words under the picture that tell what people are saying. A black band at the bottom of the screen contains the captions. The words are usually typed in white to make them easy to read.

There is no fee for getting closed captions. People do not need any special decoders if their TV set is made after 1993. To get the closed captions, people just press a button on their TV set or remote control. The captions then appear at the bottom of the screen.

The first television show with closed captions appeared in 1972. It was a cooking show called *The French Chef*. The first children's show with closed captions was called *ZOOM*. It was broadcast with captions in 1975.

Many other programs soon began to offer captions. In 1989, several music videos were broadcast with captions. This allowed deaf people to hear the words on music television channels.

Television shows that offer captions will show a special symbol at the beginning of the program. The symbol for closed caption is CC, or an icon that looks like a comic strip's speech bubble.

Earthquake! Run for cover!

CAPTIONING ON BIG SCREENS

Many foreign movies have subtitles so that viewers who speak other languages can understand them. While the actors are speaking in their own language, what they are saying is printed at the bottom of the screen for people to read.

Captioning is also used for big-screen viewing for people who cannot hear. A technique called rear-window captioning (RWC) helps hearing-impaired people to enjoy movies more. At the back of the theater is a large rear-window display. The words spoken in the movie are printed in reverse, just like in a mirror. The seats have holders for small pieces of plexiglass.

The glass reflects the words so the viewer can read them. It appears that the words are superimposed on the large screen. These pieces of plexiglass are portable so that people do not have to sit in special seats.

Many theaters now have rear-window captioning. This means that people who cannot hear can go to movies at the same time as their friends and family. RWC does not upset other moviegoers as it is silent. It also does not distract them as the sound from headsets sometimes does.

Deaf moviegoers read text captions at movie theaters equipped with RWC. The captions are reflected onto adjustable plexiglass screens from a large display screen at the back of the theater.

OTHER WAYS OF HEARING

Some hearing-impaired people have dogs to help them hear. These dogs can be any breed. They need to be intelligent and able to tell one sound from another. Hearing dogs are specially trained. Training can take from four months to one year. The dogs can be trained to respond to almost any sound. Most hearing dogs can alert their owner to up to six different sounds. When the dog hears the sound, it touches its owner and leads him or her to the sound.

Dogs can also be taught to react differently to different sounds. For example, if a smoke alarm rings, the dog can lead the owner outside to safety. If a telephone rings, the dog can bring a portable phone to the owner.

Some Sounds Hearing Dogs Can Alert Their Partners To

Alarm clock

Door knock or bell

Intruder

Person calling their name

Smoke alarm

Stove timer

Telephone ringing

Hearing dogs can make life much easier
for deaf or hearing-impaired people.

THE DEAF COMMUNITY

The deaf community has its own culture just as other groups of people do. All cultures have certain rules and customs that are understood by people in that culture. One aspect of culture is body language. Body language is different in different cultures. For example, in the Thai culture, it is important not to point your foot at someone. This is rude. In many Polynesian cultures it is not appropriate to pat people on the head. Many cultures see touching people as inappropriate.

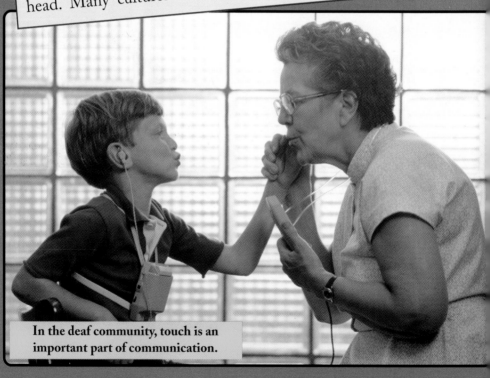

In the deaf community, touch is an important part of communication.

But this is not so in the deaf community. In this community, touch is an important way to get someone's attention.

People involved in the deaf community recognize deafness as a difference, but not a disability. As well as mixing with hearing people, they also join together to support each other. Meetings, clubs, and other activities help keep deaf people in any community in touch with each other.

INDEX

blockage 2, 5

conductive hearing loss 5, 7

congenital deafness 6, 9

culture(s) 30

development 14, 20

eardrum 3, 4

earmold 11, 12

frequency/frequencies 10

gestures 15

hearing dogs 28, 29

impulses 3, 4

operator 23

rear-window captioning 26, 27

sensorineural hearing loss 5–7

sound waves 2, 3

subtitles 26

television 25, 26

vibrations 2, 3, 7